7/16
LARRY —
FROM
LES

D0979953

dancin'

SCHMANCIN'

with the

scars

Lights – Camera – Traction!

*Finding the Humor
No Matter What!*

Jan Marshall

Copyright © 2012 by Jan Marshall

First Edition

DO WRITE PUBLISHING
Laguna Woods, California
www.authorjanmarshall.com

All rights reserved. No part of this book may be reproduced or transmitted in any form or by any means, electronic or mechanical including photography, recording or any information storage and retrieval system without written permission from the author and publisher.

Although the author and publisher have made every effort to ensure the accuracy and completeness of information contained in this book, we assume no responsibility for errors, inaccuracies, omissions, or any inconsistency herein.

Some material originally appeared in Ms. Marshall's humor columns.

Cover concept by Stanley Friedman
Design by Illumination Graphics
Photograph on back cover by Ligva Svikss

ISBN: 978-0-9885146-0-7 trade paperback
ISBN: 978-0-9885146-1-4 e-book

Printed in the United States of America

"Jan's humor and upbeat attitude before and after her brain surgery astonished us all and most likely was the key to her remarkably quick recovery."

Dr. Robert Jackson, 2005

"Laughter lightens the mood, puts things in perspective, and heals the troubled heart... The more we take ourselves lightly, the more our spirit soars. So let us age into laughter. It may be the greatest gift we can give to others, and it can also heal us"

Drew Leder, Ph.D.
From his book *Spiritual Passages*

"Wrinkles merely indicate where the smiles have been."

Mark Twain

"Humor is an affirmation of dignity, a declaration of man's superiority to all that befalls him."

Romain Gary

Someone once suggested we should all hang out with a goofy friend once in a while. Why can't that be you, *this time?*

Anonymous

DEDICATION

To Gabrielle Giffords and Mark Kelly who continue the dance with incredible spirit and laughter.

To our serving and returning wounded veterans who strive mightily to get back to the dance.

And to my dear friends below who continue to contribute enormously to our world in spite of eternal grief in losing their child:

Gigi Michaels   *Jennifer Taylor Honick*

Suzy and Paul Rosenberg   *Lisa Brett Egan*

Larry and Lillian Lipson   *Jeff (Jeffrey) Adam Lipson*

George and Anita King   *Steven*

Maxine and Don McIntosh   *Tod Randall*

Lynn Matz Ham   *Kelley Lynn Fisher*

DiAnna Shields   *Donovan Burdick*

CONTENTS

FOREWORD

Perhaps for some of us the golden age has tarnished a bit with health issues and loss and certainly we need to attend to all the sorrow and disappointments that are with us more and more.

Still, if we can embrace the basic requirements in our second and third acts, which include self-care, independence and dancing,* *as long* and as often possible, there is no doubt we can make it through with grace.

We also do not have to give a hoot to what others think of us. That alone is worth the journey over the hill as well as not having to do homework ever!

Giving verbal organ recitals of everything wrong with life and bodies keeps us in the hurting place.

Instead, we will surround ourselves with beauty in whatever form that takes, like music, art, hobbies and discount coupons.

If we can eventually discover humor in a dire situation, we probably have defeated and survived it. In the last part of the book, in a more serious tone, I recount a couple of the scars I encountered along the way when I was "Touched by an Angel in an Inappropriate Place."

The following is my way of viewing each occasion a bit differently than most rational people.

I have a congenital condition known as *Opticockyitis,* named after the doctor who first diagnosed it on a spaniel. It is an affliction causing me to observe many situations a bit left of center. I cannot help it. It is like being born with a Whoopee cushion in my head. Even when I was dealt a major blow in my life, and *after* I finished crying, moaning and kvetching (AKA complaining), my ability to observe the situation with a skewed perspective apparently saved my life, according to my physicians. In this book, I have expanded my philosophy to the point of absurdity.

Do you still feel like kvetching? Just for today, my RX is a chunk of chocolate to get to the next day. Hey, my name is *not* Pollyanna! I figure since everything passes, and with my memory, I may not recall yesterday's hassles, but I still have the chocolate bit stuck in my tooth so I will recall it as a sweet day.

* Dancin is my code for doing *anything* that gives you pleasure.

THE LIGHTER SIDE

1

ROMANCE AND SENIORS

Love is in the air. Have you been looking for love in all the wrong places?

Fear not. Help is on the way. For those not in a close romantic relationship, allow me to provide facts as to where love connections connect. The most popular meeting ground: *all* pharmacies. I overheard one man saying to a woman, while gazing soulfully into her shopping cart, "Gas and heartburn pills? Gee whiz, me too!" Burping, they waltzed to the checkout counter together.

Another whispered, "Hey babe, how would you like to soak your dentures in my Smuckers® jelly glass?"

Please be cautious, though. There is danger lurking in these drug stores. I was almost run down in the parking lot when a throng of stalkers on walkers ran after a fellow with those little blue pills. Through cataract eyes, the running gray hairs looked like dancing Q-tips.

I myself have used Internet Dating. Though much more successful than my previous attempt of singing "Love for Sale" at malls with rouged cheeks in my Anna Lucasta off-the-wrinkled-shoulder gown, it wasn't profitable. One guy offered me $2.00, but I had to pay for his parking. Actually, I have met more interesting but sometimes unsuitable characters online.

My first responder was from "Schlemiels on Wheels." He arrived on skates. His profile picture said 60. His face said 90. Looks aren't everything, and he wasn't exactly lying when he stated he was into travel and speeding, as I had to grab on to the back of his jacket as we whizzed down to a local diner for the 4 o'clock special. Honestly, I would have preferred my own skates.

My next computer catch was a Dermatologist. He wrote that famous book, *7 Solutions for Highly Itchy People*. On Valentine's Day, he bought me one long-stemmed jar of calamine lotion. I scratched him off my list.

One nutty lover wanted me to call him "Ida Lupino" during coitus.

I mentioned in one ad that I liked tall men. This one came to the door on stilts. I really liked him. I had to end the relationship 'cause I kept getting splinters in my thighs.

Ed Rex said he was close with his mom which is usually a good sign; however, I felt having her picture on the ceiling was pushing it. The relationship didn't last. Usually, neither did he.

One blind date drank his wine from a "sippy cup." It was rosé. I still can't tolerate a man who will not pick a side.

Happily, destiny intervened during my last connection, though.

I always urge all seniors to practice safe sex and I myself

usually wear a seat belt. But this one time, I did not. At the height of passion, I whispered to my partner, "Are you comfortable?" He answered, "I make a living."

I laughed so hard…

I fell off the bed…

Injured my back…so

I am now… dating my Chiropractor, who really is nice but such a manipulator!

The guy I really want to meet is Paul. Everyone is always taking from Peter to give to Paul so he must be *loaded!*

What have I deduced from my many experiences? Men only want one thing: the remote control.

So however you want to meet a date, the choices are available.

We senior people, while we all may not have great circulation, we still manage to circulate. So my personal advice is this: if you are single, gather at a pharmacy and match your prescriptions and find someone to love in sickness and *whatevah*!

2

SORRY SIRI, WRONG NUMBER

(I blame *you*, Alexander Graham Bell)

In simple times I only searched for my *other* shoe or a lost lover. Complications have now arisen.

Having been a good girl all year, while earnestly trying to reverse that reputation, my generous family bought me an iPhone 4S for Siri or *Sadist*.

Siri is called a "virtual assistant," meaning she is purported to be my own personal secretary, living conveniently in my phone, thus saving me employee salaries, insurance and wasteful café latte soy frappuccino espresso – hold the mustard – coffee breaks.

She is driving me…virtually nuts! The instructions state to speak a request as I would to a regular secretary and she will assist me. I am simply to ask her to find something or give her a reminder to remind me. We have now had horrendous arguments with lots of cursing, some of it coming from me, too.

Siri has a tone of superiority and is judgmental. When I asked her to "please (I always say *please* and *thank you*) find me a Thai restaurant nearby," she yelled, "I have no contact for your thighs and besides, we just met, so I think you are being too forward in asking me such things; as a matter of fact, you disgust me!"

So for the fourth time I reiterate that it is a restaurant that I am actually seeking. Once again she asks, "What kind of restaurant." I reply, "Thai." She says, "I do not see that in your contact list. Is there anything else I can help you with?" After 20 minutes of this banter, I change my plea to a search for the nearest bar. She wants to know if I wish to attend a Bar named Mitzvah. I fib and say, "Confirm," because hopefully they serve drinks there.

We have now started couple's therapy. My buddy thinks she is so great in making, breaking and lying about his appointments that he has asked her to marry him. She replied, "We hardly know one another. I don't see me in your contacts. I am currently seeing a few million others. Let's just be friends." Then she bad-mouthed *me*.

Another daily challenge is my attempt to locate this smartphone at least twice a day, since another one of Siri's actual tasks is to play "hide and seek." When at a public venue or in a meeting, I keep the phone on vibrate, so I am not rude to others. I know, I know. I am a good girl. However, when I return home, I occasionally forget to turn the ringer back on.

Suddenly I hear a buzz, which could be a bee or the

aftermath of that Bar Mitzvah. I then figure out it is Siri or a caller. The challenge is that in my home there are so many things that vibrate, I frankly do not know where to look for the phone.

So this is my suggestion to the next Jobs genius: Design a mini-mini GPS tracking gizmo which I can place next to my skate key and wear as a necklace.

When any gadget, including Siri, goes missing, a small voice will tell me to "look under the couch or check the icebox." Brilliant people have designed incredible devices to make life easier (except for that *bitch* Siri), so why not help out those of us who often misplace things?

If you have a better solution for searching, please call my cell phone, but do not speak to Siri, as she is a lying dog!

3

DEAR JUSTIN TIMBERLAKE

There are things you should know about this granny and other sexy old broads. True, you are used to quick Twitter messages, but since I am Twitter-less, *thus far,* I urge you to keep reading to the end where, I guarantee, before the year is over, I will get to the point.

In the past when I shouted, "Is there a doctor in the house?" in a crowded venue, it was usually to introduce him to my niece. Since she does incredibly well on her own and, in fact, has a restraining order against me for doing so, I choose now to shout that in an actual doctor's office, where they frequently keep me waiting an hour and half beyond my actual scheduled appointment.

Though my days are fully occupied searching for keys and plucking the hairs on my face, to others, sitting in a doctor's office seems wasteful. In fact, it is most enjoyable and is the only reality show I watch. The waiting areas are usually mobbed. My number, as in "Take a number and sit down, Lady," is 48, so there is time to observe.

I heard one woman mumble while reviewing her multitude of medical forms in order to be seen by a specialist, "Left nostril, heart valve, ear, buttock, pinkie toe on right foot, pinkie toe on left foot." Frustrated, she stood up and burst out in song: "All of me; why can't they take all of me?" We sympathized and hummed along. Another fellow sitting with us had been waiting so long that he called the receptionist from his cell phone *while in that very room*, wanting to speak directly to the Urologist.

She asked if he could hold, and he shouted, "If I could hold, I would not be asking for the Urologist, you &*%&%^."

He had a point. We applauded, then washed his mouth and ours as well with a Gray Goose liquid and the wait didn't bother us as much.

Go figure: when doctors were on strike, I stayed healthy. I had so much leisure time that I went to a psychic for fun. She said I would meet a tall, dark stranger...who would remove my gall bladder. I went to a palm reader for a second opinion; she removed my diamond ring.

Now, I visit actual healers. My primary doctor is a Recommendologist. Whenever I see him for any reason, he says I have a virus which is Latin for "I don't know what the hell you have." Then he recommends a specialist, usually one not covered by my plan.

So with apologies to you, Mr. Timberlake (loved you on *Saturday Night Live!*), there are differences in our movie-making style. I know what yours is and I am all for *that,* though if I made a film, I would add a bonus scene. This would feature a romantic rendezvous with a man who includes me in his health insurance plan. Now, that's what I would call a true *"Friend with Benefits."* See you at the Oscars!

4

KNOCK ON WOOD, AS LONG AS YOU ARE HEALTHY!

It was said that the safest place to be is in bed since the only accident there would result in a soft cuddly being that would take care of us in our senior years. It seems to be less of a threat recently so try not to worry.

The common wisdom is to keep active for a healthy life.

Out of the bedroom there are so many hazards with sports and exercising that one must keep a doctor on speed dial or attached to your iPad.

For seniors, white is a prominent color: the favored shade for wrapped elbows, knees and eyes because of sports injuries. When our tennis and lawn clubs require proper attire, it means bandages.

Bowling was never considered dangerous unless your fingers became stuck and you were flung down the lane with the ball. If you made a strike, it was worth the concussion. The new affliction: bowler's toe caused by stress from trying to avoid stepping over the foul line or your whiney partner's face.

The ocean's exquisite stillness and ever-present surf teach us much about life's ongoing process. Still, those senior beach boys better watch out. The danger: surfer's ear brought on by waves bouncing off their bifocals into the eardrum.

Since more people are sitting at computers all day, they get a "barrel bottom." (I believe a polka song was written for me that kept me happily rolling along). The medical term for the condition, though, is "secretary spread." If you are an executive, it is known as the high-priced spread.

I just learned of a new pain which comes from twits who tweet. It is known as twitter thumbs. If you see someone with thumbs in an upright position, it is not because they are happy to see you. Nor are they hitchhiking as one anonymous Medicare Mama did. Someone told her to please stop lifting her skirt while seeking a ride as her blue-striped stockings were causing a distraction. She was not wearing stockings. Okay, it was me. *Shaddup!!* The upright digit you see is from the frozen fingers of texting fools, including me.

We are all members of the "Dancing with the Scars" club. It is a smash, excuse the expression. Join us and line dance to our theme song, "Our Achy Breaky Parts."

5

ODE TO A SNEEZE

Preparation for the next flu incident: bathe in Purell®. Do not kiss anyone except if it is Tonto wearing a mask. Wear fashionable gloves day and night. Unless you are on your honeymoon and staying in your room 24-7, postpone hugging.

While every possible precaution must be taken to avoid this dangerous virus, I do, however, encourage you to catch a cold. Yes, my friends, the common cold is the very best thing that can happen to you. It's simply your body crying out for love.

Rarely do I see my pals cry. Sure, when they lose at golf or a caterer runs out of liver, tears do flow, but not often. That's too bad. The truth is that a cold gives one an opportunity to revert to a childish state, to be pampered and cared for. It permits the strongest people to let go without losing face, so to speak.

Here are just a couple of documented medical examples I found in my drawers.

- One board member literally strikes fear wherever he journeys. He is a tyrant and a huge trouble-maker. Yet when he is at home with a bad cold, he sucks his thumb and calls his wife "Mommy."

- An actress neighbor, who played the warden in prison films, permits her mate 24 hours to be sick; she prepares chicken soup, allows him to moan, "I'm dying. I'm dying" every hour on the hour, while rocking him in her mattress-size arms. The next day she makes the bed and pushes him out the door. This keeps him functioning for the rest of the year. He is often seen without a jacket on wintry days, stepping in puddles and sleeping with a wet head stuck out an open window praying for a relapse.

HISTORICAL FACT: The reason some battles are called "Cold Wars" is because the need for love was not met. If opposing sides could stay home and get a little cuddling...really, who feels like fighting with a runny nose?

MY ADVICE: If someone sneezes, don't just say *"Gesundheit."* Understand that this person craves compassion. Be gentle, but no kissing. Unless you yourself feel needy, then, yes, place a lip-lock.

RX: When you do catch a cold, get into a cuddly bed and collapse. You may drink liquids or not. It doesn't matter whether you stand on your head singing the Kashgaviston National Anthem; your cold will last two to seven days or as long as you need it. That's it.

Call me in the morning.

Leave your insurance information.

6

CHEDDAR CHEESE AGES, NOT US!

In my community, we are all 55-plus, except for a few trophy husbands and our Boomers Club, of which I am a proud member, though truthfully, my baby boomed a long time ago. The age is just a starting point. It's the attitude and spirit that make it one of the most popular groups.

I wonder why age is even mentioned in newspapers unless for something spectacular, like if one completes the Senior Olympics or being that 99-year-old woman who gave birth while playing tennis or the 104-year-old guy who claims to be the "baby daddy."

What purpose is served writing "Myrtle, 86, showed her works"? It is enough to say "Myrtle showed her stuff to anyone who asked." The Artist/Exhibitionist Myrtle and most residents are seasoned seniors and ageless. We are not Cheddar Cheese! Labels already exist: infants, toddlers, teenagers, adults and seniors. We don't need no more stinkin' labels.

In addition, 90 is now considered the new 70; 65 is now 50; and 40 is almost adolescent, so do any of us really know how old we are anyway? It only matters on Thursdays when we can pay $4.00 for movies.

Suppose, instead of these silly numbers, our years were called PHASES.

Years 1-40	PHASE 1
Years 41-80	PHASE 2
Years 81-120	PHASE 3

After that, name it what you wish.

Personally, I am thrilled to be in Phase 2, just like my grown children *and* Sophia Loren!

Be a pal and write Congress to make it official. About other silly body measurement numbers: if they add up to within walking distance to what they were before we shrunk, who cares?

What do you think?

7

DO NOT PUT THE BLAME ON MAME, BOYS!

If I were to spank the person most responsible for my problems, I would not sit down for a month. While I usually accept culpability for what I cause in my life, some others do not.

Recently, I went to retrieve my king-size blanket from the cleaners. Though one must allow for a bit of shrinkage, finding material the size of a pot holder seemed excessive. Attached to the little square was a disclaimer: "NOT RESPONSIBLE FOR SHRINKING, FADING, BALLING (what about bawling, mister?) OR COLOR CHANGE.

PS: EVERY EFFORT HAS BEEN MADE TO REMOVE STAINS. AS FOR THOSE REMAINING, TOUGH NOOKY, COOKIE AND FURTHERMORE, WHAT THE HELL WERE YOU *DOING* IN THAT BED?"

When leaving a restaurant, the valet brought back the car and the front seat was missing. Attached to the windshield was a card stating, "NOT RESPONSIBLE FOR ITEMS LEFT IN

THE CAR."

Television stations caution, "NOT RESPONSIBLE FOR OPINIONS EXPRESSED BY THE NEWSCASTER."

Many classified ads in the daily paper say, "NOT RESPONSIBLE FOR DEBTS INCURRED BY SPOUSE *OR* MISTRESS."

Defendants claim, *"No Mea Culpa."* Even Sinbad the Tailor has a sign that says, "NOT RESPONSIBLE FOR ALTERATIONS OR CHILDREN LEFT OVER SEVEN DAYS. "

What about the children? All this lack of accountability has filtered down to them. Show me a child who has never exclaimed, "He did it!" and I'll show you a child who was never my kid.

Yesterday I noticed my little grandson had wet his diaper. Without being judgmental, I mentioned it to him. He said, "I didn't do it."

"Who did it then?" I asked.

"Daddy did it," he replied.

I wasn't born yesterday. I know that Daddy did not do it since he was downtown in his office and that is at least 20 miles away and his car is real gas-guzzler.

Countries blame each other. Politicians accuse their opponents of messing things up. An old Spanish proverb says, "To deny all is to confess all." What the hell does that mean? Anyhow, wouldn't it be refreshing to hear one leader own up and say, "Hey guys, I goofed"?

I would stand on my head or yours, whistling while I work, just to hear one politician admit at a gathering for any cause, "The other side could actually be right, and perhaps it is only my own dark nature to see evil wherever I look. I will now stop doing that since I am (at long last) in therapy." "Therapy" is also known as "Rehab" in most circles by those wanting to avoid responsibility in actuality.

Please, enough with blaming others already. I believe most people try to do the best they can, though we can always review and improve. I vow to take full responsibility for everything in my life, except, of course, for the slight weight gain. As I have explained repeatedly at Big Girls Are Us, our theme song is "The Bigger the Figure, There More There Is to…" Well, you know. At my meeting, I have stated to the group (there are just two of us – each assigned our own personal zip code) that if one believes in reincarnation, one would know these fat cells are from my previous life when I was King George the fat, I mean the fourth, fifth and sixth. When a relative of his/mine said, "Let them eat cake," it turns out she didn't mean I should take hers.

Disclaimer: THIS PUBLISHER IS NOT RESPONSIBLE FOR ANYTHING JAN MARSHALL SAYS, EVER!

8

WHERE ARE THEY NOW?

After attending an event where volunteer clowns cheered up the evening, I had the following dream, as background circus music played and moving vans appeared.

Though many showbiz celebrities choose to live in our over-55 communities, the dream revealed our newest neighbors were from the cartoon, comic strip and fairy tale world.

I met Cinderella, recently divorced from her prince with the foot fetish. They split when she refused to wear glass shoes. Turns out he was CEO of Pyrex® and could get them wholesale, so he had a vested interest in her tootsies and those of a few of her hot friends.

She now dates Dr. Scholls®. He explained that glass slippers, unless custom-fitted with orthopedic inserts, cause bunions, not Brussels sprouts as she first thought. The Prince is now rooming with Betty Crocker® and the Pillsbury Dough Boy®. Please, don't ask!

Another truck brought Peter, Peter, that Pumpkin eater. Don't get me wrong; pumpkin itself is nutritious, but as a home, even in a dream, I guffaw. He put his wife in a pumpkin shell which happened to be in a co-op, so he could not get a reverse mortgage. While keeping her? I mean, really! I am a women's libber and I truly object to this "keeping her" business whether he keeps her "well" or not. It is simply wrong in this day and age, except perhaps at Thanksgiving.

While in sleepyland, I received an email from Goldilocks saying she wanted to move to our community but didn't have the down payment to qualify.

She lives in Hollywood over a Chinese restaurant where she grows dill. When we talked about her past, she revealed, "He was such an animal," speaking of her relationship with the papa bear. He asked her to call him "Big Daddy" at intimate moments, though that is another story for another time, perhaps never – *duh* – since she told me that in confidence as we were getting loopy at the old Brown Derby.

After Brenda Star, Ace Reporter, was fired from the newspaper beat, she moved to a senior community with her mystery man, Basil. It turns out Basil wasn't such a mystery man after all. His real name is Irving and she was mighty disappointed to learn the distinguished black patch he wore was for pink eye.

Today, a handsome man moved in next door. He was wearing blue tights. The only man I ever loved in tights was Stewart Granger in the film *Scaramouch*. I'm sure he loved me, too, though I have not heard from him recently. I wish I could tell him, "The sword wounds have healed nicely."

MY OPINION on Male Tights: NO, except if you want to learn the religion of a guy in a hurry. As for shorts: NO, No and No. What is it about older men with bad knees, arthritic joints and gorilla hair that prompt them to believe Bermuda shorts are a turn-on? To me, Yes, but the other sexy old broads do not enjoy the sight.

Meeting Red Riding Hood in a consignment store where she was selling her cape and her copy of *He's Just Not That Into You*, she confided that in the infamous court case she was questioned by a cruel, macho prosecutor.

"Why were you walking in the forest alone? Did you run out of alleys? You do know what the color red indicates, you ignorant slut, you." OMG!!!! I hate that.

Speaking of Red, a belated card from Santa insisted that Rudolph the Red-Nosed Reindeer is not an alcoholic, as some have claimed, but simply has a bad case of rosacia! (Gosh, it seems like the fake world has lots of ailments.)

I asked the new neighbor in those cute tights his name, and he said he was Superman (that's what they all say) and he sighed that his "Big S" had been retired. When he told me he was faster than a speeding bullet (been there, done that), I suggested he see a Urologist. Then I slammed the door in his face. "I Don't Get No Satisfaction" is NOT my favorite song, with apologies to fellow Medicare member Mick Jagger.

A banging noise at the door happily but confusingly awakened me. Yes, it was only a dream, but I could not fathom why I was wearing blue tights? Maybe I overdosed on chocolate and went into a coma and simply forgot why. Oh well... I see it's the cute guy with the brown shirt delivering a new book from Amazon.com: Gulliver Travels with a senior group to Europe, because if it is Tuesday, it must be…something.

9

MY COUNTRY

When I wrote this, it was an eventful, patriotic month after our brave service SEALS rid the world of that extremely bad man. The other news was that the water shortage seemed to have ebbed a bit in my community.

I have been extremely involved with conservation and recycling, even fixing my old beau up with a new friend. Other kind-hearted acts I do for this wonderful planet often occur at home where I frequently suggest to my current sweetie that we cut down on electricity.

"I'd better not cook. Let's go out to dinner. You under-stand, honey bunny, I am doing this for my country, not only for conservation but also to help the economy. Ya know, farmers, waiters, wine stewards and grape stompers and even doggie bag manufacturers need the work. It is the least I can do." I remind him.

He is doing his part as well. Whenever I start to speak, on his very own, he removes the batteries from his hearing aids. What a guy!

Saving our planet is a family matter. My granddaughter has found an ingenious way of keeping water from flowing down the drain. She soaks anything that needs washing: pots, pans, sweaters and a poodle (formerly a Great Dane). We both agree that washing items too frequently depletes water, detergent and the precious time that she could be texting on her smartphone, while I continue to try to figure how to turn *mine* on. She said soaking makes the dirt softer which is a lifelong goal on my bucket list.

My teenage grandson deserves credit as well. With his infinite wisdom, he knows not to take a bath until the Health Department issues a warning. Leave it to children to be in the know. While I was gently reminding him of the virtue of cleanliness, he, instead, was thinking of the bigger picture – remaining sooty out of concern for his country. I am so proud.

Now that the water shortage is less of an issue in my town, compared with our many other earthly issues, I revised some of my previous lists of household sacrifices.

OLD RULES

Brushing our upper teeth on Monday, Wednesday and Friday and the lower ones on alternate days: CANCELLED.

Scotch with water was not permitted during our service to our nation. Adults were required to drink straight from the bottle: CANCELLED.

I notice some of us still wish to do our part a bit longer.

There is only one edict still in place. That is the one insisting that in order to save water, we *shower with a stranger*. We have made some very good connections. We call them our "straight from the bottle" buddies, all of us proud to be Americans, all of us smelling pretty good!

10

HEY, MISTER!
YOU WANNA BUY A DUCK?

HOW IT STARTED

"SPECIAL DEAL: Barely-used television set formerly owned by a little old lady with weak eyes." These few words began my descent into the lure of garage sales.

Since then, if a sign reads "FIRE SALE" or "ONLY ONE TO A CUSTOMER," I am hooked. Today, though living in California with its relentless sun, I bought five snow tires for the price of six, because they came with a picture of snow. Because of this weakness, my own garage is overflowing with other people's discards. I am joking. In the smaller space of my retirement home, I no longer have a garage. I have an overhang, though I am exercising to remedy that. I have nightmares that my stuff is actually sitting next to my car, which is on blocks next to the broken refrigerator and the malnourished goat running wild with a refrain from the film *Deliverance* wafting by.

From my previous experiences, I have some advice if you, too, want to get rid of junk – oops – treasures.

In the beginning...buy a house with a garage. Unpack what you can. Leave the rest for when you have time. This will *never* happen. Immediately you'll have valuable items to sell at a later date.

- Check newspapers for patio and probate listings. After your partner screams at you for buying another piece of crap, you can put it away for your own big sale. Some other lady will love it. Her partner will be furious; thus, you can attend their divorce sale and buy back your stuff, plus theirs.

- Advertising is essential. Place signs on outdoor utility poles, not on your bedroom one, unless you have a lot of traffic.

- Be sure to print in bold letters "TOPLESS SALE." It will bring an abundance of people with mustaches and some men, too. That headline is not a lie. Surely you have empty jars and pots without covers.

- A description of the object must entice the customer. Example: the backless broken chair with three remaining Queen Anne legs can be turned upside down and then offered as a genuine antique "Bagel Server" from a Queen's Estate.

- Leave one item unmarked. When asked the price, say, "It is not for sale." People will plead. Stand your ground. They'll hound you: "I've just driven from Argentina for the sale." They will claim, "My astrological prediction for this day insists I purchase a leek-green loveseat like yours, lest I come to a dire end." Wait a beat...then relent and sell it to them for a ridiculously high price.

This helpful information is culled from my own experience. I fell for all of the above, so you are learning from someone knowing the ecstasy of being a customer at every flea sale, where I actually bought fleas, and the agony of not being able to find room for another "find" unless I asked my kids to move. It is not an easy decision since they are only in their forties.

I love yard sales. I'm going to watch the ads tomorrow on our local television channel. When I appeared on the air myself, pitching items our neighbors wanted to get rid of, because of my incredibly creative spiel, an unsuspecting non-advertising resident was picked up and transferred as a gigolo to another senior village. I have two cases of really old Old Spice® if he needs it.

11

NO GIFTS, I BEG YOU!

You bought me a pool table last Christmas Day.
Years ago, seats for the old Rams 49ers.
On Thanksgiving, you gave me the bird
To cook for thirty friends, plus a Shriner.
My birthday you took me away from it all.
Our room was on the eighteenth hole.
Three times I got hit with the ball.
Twice in my camisole.
Thank you kindly, but on the next occasion,
Please, listen to this sound advice.
Do not always be thinking of me.
For once, buy *yourself* something nice.
Please!

12

HOW I STOPPED SMOKING

Many, many years ago (last century when Sir Walter Raleigh and I dated), I was a smoker. I relinquished my habit reluctantly because of a few rotten kids who lived with me. They said it was wrong for me to yell at them when they ate junk food because they'd only get cavities or lose their teeth, but I would lost my life. How can you argue with such childish logic?

Even though I was never a heavy smoker – heavy came later – quitting was difficult. I adored smoking those long, slim, sexy brown cigarettes. It was all I could think of. I went to bed praying I'd awake to find it was healthier than jogging. (Hey, it happened to wine and chocolate!) I purposely burnt the food (okay, so it wasn't always on purpose) just to smell the smoke.

Then I ate everything – without pause. This is more than psychological. A cigarette is like the period at the end of a sentence. Without it, the sentence would ramble. Similarly, a meal without a cigarette to punctuate it continues eternally. So I became a researcher, not for me, mind you, but the rest of humanity. I learned that Baskin-Robbins® truly did have 32 flavors in *all* their branches. The next detective work was never conclusive. I never learned whether M&Ms® melted in my hands, my mouth or my pocket since they were gone quick as a flash. I just knew I loved them. The only foods that I was partial to were those that were sweet, sour, spicy or bland, though I did learn to enjoy solidly frozen as well.

I started eating tons of mints, chewed gum and chomped on anything not moving. Eventually though, the craving subsided because it was more of a habit than an addiction for me.

So posting grotesque photos of very ill patients on a cigarette pack or on a TV screen will not deter people, even brilliant ones who certainly know the consequences but are addicted and unable to stop on their own. They need an intervention, therapy and our compassion.

Take a smoker to lunch; though if they take out a cigarette during the meal, slap them silly. Then give them a hug!

I do not want to be judgmental. Because if they put pictures of M&Ms® on a cigarette package, who knows who could revert to earlier times?

13

WHY CAN'T WE ALL GET ALONG?

All families have conflict. We love, we hate, we eat *and* we get heartburn. So it is with my Mac and PC. Have you noticed that even among friends there exists a rivalry that includes gunfire between competing computer fanatics?

Like my computers, each thinks the other is superior. My computers in particular refuse to play nice. I loved them both as I do all my children. Mac was my firstborn, so perhaps I did favor him – maybe it's the Apple cheeks, but I'll deny this in any court. (And between you and me, our little Palm wasn't planned, but that is another story I'd rather you keep quiet about since I am not even sure who the baby daddy is. Maybe it's that 104-year-old guy.)

Nevertheless, as the purported adult here, my job was to keep my computers compatible. We had started family therapy with the Gates/Jobs Mental Nut Case Unit. Since even *they* refuse to speak with one another, what hope was there for my two? The Therapist stuffed a hard drive in her ear and has taken to heavy drinking.

My fear is if they can't get along, what chance for resolution is there for a 1440-dpi printer or for the Middle East? Okay, I am going to tell you the truth. I did love my Mac more than life itself. It was so easy to use. Yes, it was a favorite child and when I tell you why I even own a PC, you'd be astonished.

It started on one dark and stormy night while I watched a shopping channel. All I know is that they featured this cute little HP PC. Should have said "NO!" To sweeten the pot, it came with a built-in swimming pool and a closet organizer who would live with me. The best part: it was free! I only had to pay for shipping, for which I took out a bank loan.

It worked for a few years. Then, after a while, it bombed as the Mac had, and it was necessary to purchase a new machine.

Since that fateful day, I continually consider either jumping out the window or throwing out the Window (7).

I have a hate/hate relationship attempting to learn this new Word program. I had MS Word 2003 and that was fine all of these years.

Now I am in a forced relationship. This new computer was already installed with MS Word 2007. It is like a foreign language and the simplest task takes me a week. By the time I figured how to type and edit a simple congratulations note to a pair of newlyweds, they had split and were arguing over custody of their kids and their own computers.

Still, I love most new technology.

My fickleness has surfaced again. Everyone in my circle has an iPhone. (I am so jealous I have turned green) and, of course, I covet the newest Mac which is so simple it has an all-infant tech line giving instruction, plus it actually irons shirts, too.

But now my documents and forthcoming book manuscripts are on the PC, and I do not have the dough to buy a pickle, much less an Apple.

Perhaps I shall return to my old Royal Typewriter which I actually made into a lamp in my old "find uses for old crap" phase and is now lighting up my living room!

Does anyone happen to have any old black ribbon in their junk drawer? I have a publishing deadline.

14

YES, I SHOT MY SCALE, BUT I SHOT IT IN SELF-DEFENSE, SHERIFF

It is that time of year when I say, "Fat, fat go way; appear instead on Doris Day." I do not want to sue for libel, but my lying scale, which continually hides when it sees me – *yes it has bullet holes but they were blanks* – has conspired with my mirror to distort my adorable body and smooth-skinned face.

Another year, another ton more or less and I start my usual fitness/starving activities. Last year I was encouraged while jogging as I thought I heard applause. It turned out to be my thighs hitting together. Neighbors paid me to scram because the sound registered 9 on their Richter scale. It was just a few dollars (and the threat of bodily harm from residents) but it was the first time I turned flab into dollars. Now, when I am low on cash and living beyond my seams, I may run in more expensive neighborhoods. Malibu Colony, watch out.

Fitness experts advise us to set a goal in our minds. I visualize a couch or a hammock or anything I can fit my butt on. Past exercises consisted of jumping to conclusions and wrestling with my conscious. Yet, I stayed at the same weight.

Here are diet tips that turned me into a tall, thin blonde. Wait, that's someone else. Oh, I really must go to the Optometrist.

Eat as much spaghetti as you want within two minutes with one chopstick – standing on your head, of course.

Enjoy unlimited Double Fudge Chocolate Triple Decker Pecan Pie any week a politician or athlete does not cheat on his wife and/or mistresses.

CAUTION: Do not get too thin.

REMEMBER: Mirrors (who are in cahoots with scales) notoriously lie. You are beautiful and incredibly huggable.

MOST IMPORTANTLY: Consider the recession and help improve the economy. Do not diet. If you do, you will put poor little chickens and their owners out of business. Eating is good. So, let's meet at my favorite hangout. If only they hadn't named it The ELEPHANT Bar®.

15

DATE NIGHT
OR ME AND MY
MECHANICAL MAN

At a Book Faire, while sitting with talented authors pitching and wooing, a raffle was announced.

Since I am a very lucky lady, and was the first Miss America to work the pole, having repaired telephone wires in a previous life, this was just another in a list of good fortunes I experienced since becoming an oldie but goodie.

My heart pounded when I won a mechanical man. I recently read that synthetic human cells were being created in laboratories and I was in heaven. At last! There would be no more Internet dating for me. I could not wait to shave my legs and changed the sheets.

Shocked, I soon learned the raffle was for a gift to a *Mechanical Mann* automotive service. I was grateful, particularly since my recent experience with a car repair shop had been dismal. This is what transpired when I drove into that *other* shop.

"Well it really hurts me to tell you this, Miss, but you have diminishing pressure. You appear to have corrosion around your terminals and obviously your condenser is shot to hell."

I thought he was terribly rude and wondered why he didn't also mention my weight gain while he was insulting me.

"What about the car?" I asked.

"There are no guarantees in life. I'll do what I can."

"How much will it cost?" I muttered.

"How much do you have?" I thought I heard him whisper.

"There are no guarantees (*again* with the no guarantees) but I estimate from – hmm, let's see – from who-knows-what to $1,600."

"I don't get it. It is one stinkin' brake light," I started to object.

"Mama, you just don't know anything about electrical systems or about cars. You should bring a male with you next time. They never question my judgment, because they are *manly*. Guys know stuff that little ladies do not. So go get a facial (another insult) and tell your fellah to come in without you."

I backed out and accidentally ran over his foot. Instinctively, I called him a dipstick, not actually knowing what that was, but suddenly I felt relieved.

I purchased a car repair manual. The first time I glanced under the hood I fainted. Who knew there were so many parts? Then I learned that cars have a simple and organized system.

Previously, I thought if a belt was broken, my pants would

fall down. Now I know it could be a belt from the water pump or a vast number of things.

I learned that when my engine knocks, I no longer ask, "Who is there?"

As it turned out, the solution for my car was a new bulb which was quite reasonable.

I also realized while it is good to be informed, I prefer to let honest experts handle their specialties. Thus, my old Lexus coupe and I will be regulars at a certified dealer. Talk about lucky (*L'amour*, which is actually my stage name), I truly love being a grey-haired type. You'll notice I said "type." Only Clairol® and I know the whole truth about the curtains matching the drapes.

But I digress once again. While I do appreciate winning that prize, an actual mechanical man would have solved so many other problems. But truthfully, when it comes time to rotate my tires, there is nothing like a real man.

16

BEN FRANKLIN'S MOTHER WAS A NAG, TOO

DISCOVERED IN A SENIOR COMMUNITY

TO: BENJAMIN FRANKLIN
FROM: YO MOMMA
DATE: JULY 5, 1776

Benji, why haven't I heard from you? While you were signing all those declarations, and had the quill out, couldn't you drop me a line? I received your thank-you note for the Chinese urn, but I hoped for a real letter. Not that your letters are always cheerful. Why do you still resent being one of fifteen children? So you had to wear hand-me-downs. So? Your sister isn't that much bigger than you. If you're so smart, why didn't you tell your father that an ounce of prevention was worth – well, never mind.

Ben, there are a couple of things I want to talk to you about. I heard you were seen in Congress last week wearing those stupid tiny spectacles called Granny Glasses? Are you a Granny? No! So stop it! Get something more fashionable. Speaking of luck, you are pushing yours. Everyone knows about your little escapades. If you're not careful, your wife – what's-her-name – is sure to find out. I've learned about the new one you're sneaking around with, Penny Pupnik. Ben, listen to your mother, I'm telling you for your own good. The next time you are with her and you hear your wife approaching, you'd better hide her in the vase. Believe me, a Penny urned is a Penny saved. Oh, stop groaning.

Speaking of smashing, that's exactly what I wanted to do to your nose after I read your latest remark, "When man and woman die as poets have sung, his heart's the last that moves; her last the tongue." That was so typically choov...Chauvin... shavinis – well, you know what I mean. One more slur like that and you'll have to change the name of your almanac to "Poor Benny's." By the way, there is no "k" in the word "almanac," sweetheart.

I'm worried about your instability. You have been a cartoonist, a printer, an editor, an inventor, a scientist, a philosopher, a statesman ... I mean, how do you think that looks on your employment application in these tough times? Frankly, Benji, I think you need counseling, which is the actual purpose of this letter.

I've learned about a wonderful new therapy group. I'm sure you'll benefit from it. A couple of the people attending may be in worse shape than you, believe me, so you needn't be shy. One of them, Marie Curie, insists on being called "Madame," of all things. Anyway, her husband persuaded her to attend the meeting because she cannot cook worth a darn. He says, every time she goes into the kitchen, he hears pots rattling and things bubbling on the fire, but when he asks, "What's for dinner?" she says, "Nothing!" It is driving him nuts. Then there's a man named Morse. What a nervous Nelly he is! Can't sit still for a minute without tapping his fingers – on tables, chairs, anything he gets his hands on. Just don't sit next to him unless you need a massage.

I think this twelve-stepper would be good for you. Listen, Benji, I only want you to find yourself – to be happy. Perhaps, if you listen to your mother, you'll amount to something. Most of all, remember what you yourself told me. "If a man empties his purse into his head, no one can take it from him…" Need I say more? Get help!

Love, Mummy.

17

CLUTTER SCHMUTTER

What do ribbons, yo-yo's and dental floss have in common? They are all knotted together in the same drawer in a dwelling known as Fibber and McGee Manor.

While I have a place for everything, I do not really know where that place is. I long for a day when every item in the universe has its own beeper that I can click on to appear in the room that *I* am in.

When I do find something that looks familiar, I am clueless as to what it is for. On the coldest day of winter, when the heater key is gone, I remember that item but not where I put it. But I am sure it is safe. And I have a blanket I wear backwards so I do keep warm.

I truly love order. I crave it. But what can I do when the alien devils that come in the dark of night sneak in and throw newspapers and assorted documents around my place?

I am truly fed up with putting the same stuff away. A recent magazine survey asked women how they felt about housework.

The majority said "Bleckkk!" The others were too weak from laughter to respond. It is like asking a turkey how he feels about Thanksgiving.

Straightening up is like putting beads on a string without a knot at the end. It is an endless job. So in order to get through maintaining order, I developed timeless stress-relieving techniques. I suggested these to Martha Stewart as well so she can finally take a bathroom break.

- Dusty tables are great for writing $#%^& words on. When you hear guests approach, simply shake your booty or feather duster to delete the offensive language. Both you and your guests will be relieved and you will be exercising as well as polishing furniture.

- If you neglect to polish silver for eight years it begins to look like pewter. Pewter is very nice.

To those judgmental folks, my kindhearted explanation: papers piled high, documents hither and yon, scattered clothing and topless jars are being sorted to send to the poor people who have lost everything playing Bingo.

What can I do? It is just my nature. Please address thank-you notes to Saint Jan.

Oh, I suggest the next time you visit me, forget the hostess gift. Instead, please bring me a pair of thigh-high boots. It's just a silly Health Department thing. But *really*...bring them!

18

SHINE YOUR HEAD
IN MY DIRECTION

Toupee or Not Toupee
That is the question.
Whether it is nobler to
Suffer the eagle's droppings,
Yet pray for the Slings and Arrows of one tiny
sparrow
Or be transplanted and screw
One's courage to the sticking place.
Ah! Men at some time
Are Masters of their fate,
But, nay, not when misfortune
Strikes their balding pate.

Men are going bald at an earlier age because balding men are advanced human beings.

Years ago, cave men and others needed hair all over their bodies because they were Neanderthals (generally a lost species except for my last date) but now they don't need the hirsute look because our earth is warmer, we have central heating, and many of our guys mostly do stand upright when sober.

Still, there are a few men who insist on covering their heads with discarded carpet patches or actual bird's nests. PLEASE STOP IT! We know. WE KNOW! This artificial turf looks nothing like what Mama Nature originally provided. Have mercy on the little homeless bluebird who cannot find his house since you stole it.

I understand it is usually a male thing, though it can affect women, too.

So I implore you: if you must cover yourself, please go to a trained wig maker or hair stylist who can assist you. Since you go to a specialist for your big toe and every other body part, why plop a mop on top when you have a need for cover? Let an expert help you look like the original handsome hunk you were.

But, before you do go to a professional, I urge you to first consider this: BALDING MEN ARE BETTER LOVERS! It has something to do with the energy that was formerly generated by the electricity found in hair follicles. When the hair is gone, the energy has to find a place to park, so it goes to the libido and hangs around there.

There is a practical matter as well, in being a beautifully bodacious bald man. Consider the money saved on shampoo and conditioner. So your lady can't run her fingers through your hair but she could slip and slide. In the evening, your head can be used as a nightlight and, perhaps with a little buffing, a makeup mirror. "Honey, please shine your head in my direction. I want to check my lipstick."

The best idea is to accept your condition and to understand that your shiny heads look terrific. If your hair is just beginning to thin out, do not worry. Trust me. It will all come out all right – probably on my pillow.

19

THE FELON AND THE FUZZ

This is Jan, felon # 949. Here is *my* version of the notorious incident.

THE CRIME: Gorgeous Officer Krupke claimed, according to his toy ray gun, that I was zooming more than 30 mph in the 25-mile zone of a senior community. It only appeared that I was racing. There is a tricky, unexpected hill heading down the street to the post office, an obvious speed trap. My speedometer showed a tad *less* than 30 mph. Perhaps the icy, snowy roads accounted for the excess. Hey, it could happen in sunny California someday!

Being innocent, I decided to fight this injustice. I pleaded my case at our Traffic Dispute Court headed by two friends. They claimed they had no power to sentence me but felt free to utter "Tsk, Tsk" about my crime repeatedly.

ASSISTING CALIFORNIA'S ECONOMY: To save the state money for my possible incarceration, I arrived at my hearing with tattoos of wrinkles in place and a stylish striped jumpsuit from Armani. Though I hadn't received a traffic ticket outside of this area in over 45 years, it mattered not to this tough jury.

I warned my grandkids that I could be sent to the big house. Initially they thought it was swell, imagining it would be larger than my own and thus better for playing hide and seek. They agreed finally that I was only guilty…of loving them too much.

Their cries of "Puleez…free Granny Janny" broke my heart.

My attorney was absent. He is in jail for money and underwear laundering, both not belonging to him. I believe my arrest was a scam. Handsome Officer Krupke issues tickets and then pitches his very own traffic class. I smell corruption and Old Spice. I would also like to know why I wasn't manhandled by Handsome Officer Krupke as my neighbor George had been during the same day of the event. Reverse discrimination is still discrimination.

THE VERDICT: I was found guilty of wanton speeding while wonton eating.

MY SENTENCE: Either pay an enormous fine (possibly leading to a real crime of robbing banks) or attend his class for senior delinquents. I chose the traffic school – a sleep-inducing two hours. To keep awake, one guy bounced on a pogo stick while another shaved his wife's back. After the longest morning of my life, I vowed to go straight.

Though who can actually predict the future? Since getting my newest tattoo, "Born to Be Sorta Wild If My Arthritis Doesn't Act Up," it is possible some day – if I can *still* reach the steering wheel – I may go crazy and drive 32 miles mph. NASCAR, call me!

20

HOLIDAY HUMBUG

I am simply pooped from partying in and out of my home. I have attended or hosted so many events and was force-fed so much food that I am fatter than a bloated blimp.

True, some of the bashes were bombastic.

The A party had the Aesops (she wore Sable), Al and Alice Alonzo from Albany who sold Apples and Absent-Minded Albert who forgot his pants. All in all, the A's were amiable.

At the B party, there were the Baklavas who were sweet, Bill Blasé who came alone but didn't care and Boobs Burkewitz who arrived with a couple.

Now I owe so many reciprocal invites, which will then lead to more invitations till infinity, that I had to find a way to end the cycle. I have created sure-to-discourage themes guaranteeing nobody will return a second time. From my recent experiences, you, too, can learn how to make sure you are left alone, *if* that is your wish.

THE SURPRISE PARTY

Hide 10 people in a closet when the evening is warm and

sticky. Make everyone whisper for an hour, drinks in hand. When the honoree arrives, everyone will be so zonked they will ignore him. He'll leave thinking he is in the wrong house. Who cares?

THE BUFFET

Place small throw pillows on the floor for guests to sit on so they must balance their plates on their laps or someone else's. Serve cracked crab with drippy hollandaise sauce, corn on the cob and huge Margaritas. Make an obscene remark which will embarrass the most sophisticated guest, who will then spit and splatter everyone. Do not worry about being asked to *their* home.

DO IT BY PHONE; KEEP THE DESSERT FOR YOURSELF

"Hi Mona, can you believe it's already a year since we celebrated my mother-in-law's hip replacement? Oh, you can't make it. So sorry, sweetie." (Ha!)

For the future, unless it is a small dinner party (count on me for the whine), or we can meet in a restaurant, leave me alone and I sure won't bother *you*. My guarantee – if the phone doesn't ring, you'll know it's me.

Happy Holidays or whatever!

21

THIS GIRL'S BEST FRIEND

Shoeless, I gracefully frolic as neighbors lovingly walk their pups, baggies in hand.

I want you to know I appreciate you all.

No animals do more for people than dogs. (I do not want to hear from monkey lovers, *puleez!*) Dogs have existed for centuries, protecting and pooping on property. Indeed, the ancient Ethiopians respected dogs so much they once chose a dog as king. They obeyed his every command, or what they believed to be his will, whenever he barked.

They must have been busy, those Ethiopians, if their king was anything like our dog. He barked at cat commercials and vacuum cleaners. Ants drove him nuts. He adored burglars. He allowed us to sleep throughout the night while two bikes and a weed whacker were snatched.

An Intelligence Test for Dogs attempted to convince me our dog was not too bright. Tests, like elections, are open to interpretation. Some say my dog had a bird brain, but I see him as having different priorities from us. Insects bug him; burglars do not.

Fortunately, he never learned he was too good for us. We already felt inferior since he was a purebred. We were mutts from Brooklyn. His name was Charlton Farthington Worthington IV. I teasingly called him Chuck.

Environment is said to influence canine behavior. Not true. He was brought up to believe that sex is beautiful, a natural function between consenting adults. Still, the few times a year that he'd slink out the doggy door and hook up with the poodle/slut next door wearing her off-the-shoulder flea collar, Chuck returned filled with guilt. He'd sneak across the floor close to the wall and hide under the bed. Where did he learn that? We hadn't behaved that way in years, since long before his arrival.

If Chuck flunked an IQ test, I'd still adore him. He was loyal, forgiving and licked us all over when we returned home. Can you make that statement about any other friend? Do you have his number?

22

MIND-BODY VERSUS GIRTH CONTROL

In spite of my fight with the scale and frequent attempts to be slender, I realized I needed a new snack – I mean *tactic*.

I finally decided to host my own peace accord. Pressuring me to get in shape never worked since my mind and body were never on the same plate.

Both consider the other an enemy and have fought constantly. I was fed up. It was time for a truce.

Communication was all it took. I recorded it for you.

MIND: Well Bod, this is truly an historical event. For the first time we are involved in "peaceful negotiations" toward a just and lasting thinness.

BODY: Yes, we have always had the same objective which was to cut calories. It was the method that caused those belly skirmishes. I am pleased we are finally talking steps in unison towards a fabulous figure.

MIND: I agree, Body, and that is why I'd like you to know that I acknowledge your right to exist (although I question the amount of territory you cover).

BODY: Just listen to that! She recognizes my right to exist. The audacity!

MIND: Now you listen. No need to revert to your old hostile manner.

BODY: I would like to remind you that I am not hostile but I definitely do not need your permission to exist. I just do and that's that. What I would prefer, actually, is to get back to the bargaining table, which just happens to be in the kitchen. Would you like some fruit and cookies?

MIND: Of course not! After all, the point we are attempting to agree on is how you are going to drop a few pounds. Now the question is, "What are you willing to give up in order to gain these results?"

BODY: Hey, we are in this together. Let's take back our good looks together. Also, do not use the word "gain" in my presence. If we agree, in order to live in harmony with you, I'd relinquish the nutty peanut butter I smear on my Sara and Tommy Lee Pounds of Cake. Believe me, that is some sacrifice. So! What will you do in exchange?

MIND: How about no more scolding? I won't remind you a moment on your lips is forever on your hips, thighs* and chins, both of them. And I promise not to say you are a bad person when you finish the kid's leftover dinner each night *considering he is not your kid or even sitting at your table.*

BODY: Good. Because the more you yelled, the worse I felt,

and the worse I felt the more I ate. I am convinced you are sincere in your wish to reach a lasting "sveltness." Let's celebrate with a brief interruption in our talks and order pizza.

MIND: Pizza! How can you consider pizza at a time like this?

BODY: Okay, forget the pizza. How about spaghetti?

MIND: Spaghetti is out of the question.

BODY: What if I promise to jog, clog and tap-dance every day?

MIND: No!!! There is no way spaghetti is acceptable if we are to arbitrate reconciliation.

BODY: Then that is just too bad. I will never, ever give up spaghetti. If you accept my pasta position, I will adhere to other conditions. What if I stop lying about my height?

MIND: No! If our goal is to keep you/us from looking like a double-decker bus, then we must give up spaghetti, and that is that!

BODY: Never!!!!

MIND: Well, I am afraid we can no longer keep up these talks.

BODY: Please. Do not close the door to peace completely. Why don't we find ourselves a good-humored man for a couple of scoops of chocolate-pecan with cherries?

MIND: Two scoops! Are you nuts?

BODY: Okay, okay. We'll just have one scoop.

MIND: Well, okay. You've got yourself a deal, Body Buddy. *La Chaim!*

*Historical Side Bar: Thighs with ridges were called "pulkes." Traced back to the original tribes of the Cellulites** referred to the indents as either love dimples or dumplings, since they were so into food. Before each battle, the ongoing question was, "So what do you think they'll serve at the Inquisition Café Deli?"

**Distant relatives of the Clitorians (see my forthcoming book, "Stretch Marks: Ageless Wisdom for Sexy Old Broads."

UH OH, THE SERIOUS STUFF

(How it all began)

23

TOUCHED BY AN ANGEL IN AN INAPPROPRIATE PLACE

IN THE BEGINNING, though they claim they never promised us a rose garden, they never said there wasn't one, so I assumed some time I'd wake up and there it would be. I believed it until someone up there said, "Hey pal, wanna to learn some great lessons?" Before I could answer, I endured grief, pain, illness (a real couple of lulus) including the cancer I am going to tell you about, and more recently and successfully, brain tumor surgery, plus some bad fish.

Fortunately, to repeat what I mentioned earlier, I have a congenital condition known as Opticockyitis named after the doctor who first diagnosed it on a spaniel. It is an affliction causing me to observe every situation a bit left of center. I cannot help it. It is like being born with a Whoopee cushion in my head. Whenever I was dealt a major blow in my life, and after I finished crying, moaning and kvetching, my ability to observe the situation with an unusual perspective saved my life.

But I have a confession to make. After I was touched by an angel, in an inappropriate place I was truly shocked. I said, "Not me, not cancer. Not my beautiful breast." Oh, so very *mistakenly,* I believed that women who were victim types, quiet little mice who did not assert themselves, were the ones who got cancer. I was a big mouth assertive liberated lady who couldn't possibly become one of those people. I had a mammogram every year, ate well, jogged, practiced yoga, danced, laughed and made love frequently, sometimes at the same time (talk about multi-tasking or A.D.D) so I certainly would be immune.

I had up till that point a most magnificent marriage that lasted a quarter of a century. Life had been great for the two of us stemming from a blind date and then with the three children we were blessed to have. We began with nothing but our enchanting love. He ultimately became a giant in the advertising business and I wrote satire and a weekly newspaper column, always as a-stay-at home mom.

Fast forward. After ending this union which was still the most painful but a necessary choice of my life, it brought with it the most unbelievable grief. With the help of my adult children and friends, I started on the road to the strange new land of the singles.

I needed to earn a living in the outside world. I ran humor seminars and gave motivational presentations to major corporations after my first book, "Still Hanging in There," was published. This news about cancer was a shocker. I was considered very knowledgeable in the field of humor, healing and lightening up others in the business and healing community and taught about the connection between mind and body. I stressed using humor as an important element. In workshops, I insisted that increasing the laughter in one's life was essential to one's well being. This led to many radio and television appearances including the hosting of my own cable series with the unbelievable help from my brilliant colleagues from Women in Film. That is when, among other fabulous talented people, I met the most wonderful Steve Allen. His appearance on my show was the favorite and most requested repeat segment. I then became a frequent guest on his WNEW syndicated radio show.

So, I did not fit any of the statistics, not one. At the time, no one in my family had had cancer. The direst statistic, the one about the importance of early detection did not apply, *unfortunately.* It seems that my radiologist made a major error: He had not noticed the cancer during the last two mammograms in the fourteen years he was my doctor.

This was the beginning of a situation that became increasingly worse with every moment, with every call and every decision. The fact is that before the diagnosis of cancer and that lousy chemotherapy, I was a healthy lady. It's not the illness itself, but the treatment of the toxic medications that can do you in. Years ago, applying Chemotherapy was like dropping a bomb to catch a fly. Yes, you would kill the insect, but you could also destroy everything close by as well. I know in fifty years we will look at placing toxins in our bodies as a barbaric solution to healing, just the way doctors used to remove limbs as a way to cure disease. "You must be kidding. You mean in the twentieth century when people had a severe illness, they just removed the part with the problem and then they pumped your body with crap? Wow, how disgusting is that?"

When I was told I needed a biopsy, I asked if it mattered if I waited a couple of weeks. It was 1989. I had a speaking engagement in Washington, DC. I also scheduled a meeting with Patch Adams in Virginia who is that remarkable physician who used humor in dealing with his patients and dreamt of building a hospital where there were no fees so no one was turned away.

We shared information. I told him about my planned project for placing humor/healing rooms in hospitals and corporations to begin with and then moving on to schools and community centers.

I had designed a plan to promote healing by inducing positive emotions in a hospital setting in addition to other medical therapies. It was intended to prevent burnout among hospital staff and particularly as a pleasant waiting area for visitors. Placing specific rooms with healing colors, soothing sound, ergonomically designed furniture and of course, lots of humor in every form for patients and families is an incredible healing tool.

Think of your body as a television set and your mind as a (remember them?) DVD player. You can play anything you want and it will appear on your screen, so watch what you put in that machine. A horror or destructive film or belief, so to speak, will show in the body.

Humor, on the other hand, impacts many body systems. According to Dr. William Fry, the pulse rate is higher, the heart beats faster and the arteries open up, therefore having a direct effect on the immune system.

Enlightened physicians would write a prescription for the patient to spend thirty minutes in the Humor Room just as they would prescribe a sitz bath or any other physical therapy.

The first place was to be the "Steve Allen Humor Room." Steve had become a dear friend. He was a kind, brilliant and unbelievably funny man. Tragically he died unexpectedly. So did my interest in Humor Rooms. Perhaps I will pursue that dream once more.

Yes, the doctor assured me it would be okay to take my trip, if I agreed I would not wait more than those two weeks. I took healing tapes with me to play in my hotel room as well as books and soothing meditations. I was confident that I would be okay. I have always believed in the power of prayer, the use of meditation and the kindness of strangers.

Not so fast Tomashito, as my grandma used to say, "Man plans while God laughs so hysterically." When I returned home my oldest son, Matt, a gentle man who was very concerned but only showed support, took me for the biopsy. As soon as I woke from the anesthesia, the doctor, Eva Braun was her name, blurted out, "You have cancer!" Not even an offer of a Martini with lots of olives or a slow hemming and hawing, but immediately gave me that devastating pronouncement. She said it without any compassion or softness as if she had to spit this foul taste from her mouth.

She took me to the waiting room and my son just held me close and let me cry. The doctor told *him,* I needed surgery as soon as possible.

I went for another opinion, choosing a breast center where they specialize in this type of thing exclusively. I kept imagining the elevator buttons were nipples and the love seats in the lounge were two comfy breasts. The place concentrated solely on the disease of cancer of the breast. It was there that I learned that since my cancer had existed for a long while, surgery was not only mandatory but urgent. What? How could that be? I was informed it had been there at least two years and had not been found by my trusted radiologist.

I would have preferred trying alternative methods using nutrients and other healing techniques. I wanted to be a partner in my own treatments. But the pressure was enormous from family, friends and doctors, including those who were generally holistic in their approach, for me to agree to immediate surgery. There wasn't time because of the misdiagnosis earlier, I was told.

Depending on the outcome, chemotherapy was the only game in town at that time. Due to the original error, the disease had spread to the Lymph node area.

No, no, I thought.

Yes, yes.

More interviews with doctors, one to remove the cancer, one to reconstruct the breast using the muscle and tissue from my abdomen since I did not want any foreign implants in my body. Because I was so large-breasted I would have had to use a queen size mattress anyway. The surgeon's fee was so exorbitant that I asked if he would donate part of his *huge* backside to me. Strangely, he refused. He wondered if I'd like to reduce the size of the healthy breast to match the mastectomy reconstruction. Yes, I thought but first what about the *possibility* of losing sensation in that breast, which is a highly erogenous zone, with a connecting sensation from tit to clit for me. He said casually, there was no way of knowing beforehand and we had to take our chances.

I asked how he'd feel if *we* cut just the tiny tip of his penis, (you know, the good part) and he covered himself squirmed, muttering, "bleck!" I think that meant "No." He did not understand. I chose to forgo the reduction.

Well, friends, it turned out that because of node involvement, there *was* need for chemotherapy for six months. Feeling so utterly unwell, I could not read, sleep or eat. I was throwing up constantly. My hair fell out on the pillow and in the shower. My eyebrows and lashes disappeared.

GOOD NEWS: Some hair grows back.

BAD NEWS: Some of it grows back on your face.

I saw a body that was no longer mine and a face I did not recognize. I cried every single day as I showered. Then I became a chubette. I did not know that chemo causes weight gain in many women. When the hormones stop functioning and the thyroid starts serious napping, you can exercise till Richard Simmons eats McFries every hour on the hour and still the huggable frame remains.`

I suppose you'd like me to tell you all the astonishing gifts cancer brought me, that I finally got in touch with my feelings or learned how to laugh or realized how precious life is. In fact,

I knew all that before and practiced living that way. Indeed, humor and positive thinking was my mantra and life's work. Norman Cousins and I shared research and he became a member on the board of my International Humor and Healing Institute, as were Steve Allen and notable physicians.

We all agreed that cancer or any illness is simply the life force gone wrong. It is also random. That is not to say that the losses, even dealt-with losses, do not provide fertile ground for microbes to settle and grow. They do. I had a grief of enormous proportion when I ended my marriage though I had felt I had mourned deeply. But the cells hold secrets and pains sometimes not known to the conscious mind.

Still, that could not explain the epidemic of all kinds of cancers spreading. Perhaps it is environmental, or in the foods we process or car fumes or cell phones. No one really knows yet, so please do not question people who are going through this harrowing experience. Don't ask; do it. Bring food, clean their home and take them out for fun. Am I nagging? Well Plato was a Nag, Too!©

Incurring illness, usually no one is to blame. Yes, diet, exercise and a good attitude plus supportive friends and family add to one's wellbeing. I did and had all that plus yearly mammograms. Not one woman in my family had breast cancer. Then one day... cancer appeared. I do know that all disease comes up to be heard and healed. After the screams and tears perhaps my pain was there to learn the lesson of the pain. They say that pains are gifts in disguise. I have learned much more from the pain than the good stuff. But enough with the &*&$@$#% gifts already. Stuff happens. I got it!

The drugs caused hairlessness all over; (shine *your head in my direction, baldy)* and a body that was not familiar. I cried so much.

I needed a plan for myself. So I went deep into my spiritual books from many sources highlighting anything that touched me.

I learned to say "I totally trust where I am" (in pain, sorrow or whatever); that is how one can get through anything. It is the resistance or unacceptability that keeps us from moving forward. I was depressed. I tried a new affirmation. "I accept where I am now and I don't like it one friggin bit?" That helped me.

I learned to achieve a kind of acceptance. That allowed me to see things from a different perspective. Accepting seems to be from a higher place. I needed to contribute to others. I started "Jan's Army" and sent courage badges and encouragement to those who had bravely endured and survived this awful disease.

I searched for lightness everywhere. I realized in between the threads of pain in one's life, *not a shred of evidence truly exists that life is actually serious!*

ACCEPTING IT ALL

24

ACCEPTANCE

WHAT WE NEED IS A NEW INTERPRETATION OF IT ALL. Yes, disease comes up to be heard and healed. It is the resistance or unacceptability that keeps us from moving forward.

Try a new affirmation: "I totally accept where I am (of course I'd rather be dancing), but I do totally accept where I am now and I don't like it one frigging bit, but so what?"

Actually affirmations are little Post-its® for the mind, just a reminder to keep us going as long as we realize deeper work is needed.

Never deny any type of emotional pain or it will show up elsewhere on the body or in a car crash or other mishaps.

Accepting others where *they* are or who *they* are, is not easy, but with practice the rewards are enormous.

No matter the angst, always say, "I want to see this from a higher place." Can't do that yet? Picture a ladder to get there. It will make you chuckle and you will be on your way to some kind of enlightened interpretation.

To be clear, during illness, while attitude is everything, it is not a substitute for competent medical care but it is a vital partner.

Prayer and meditation are important. Our prayers are the request, the meditation the answer, though we rarely receive what we want but as Mick (*that* role model) Jagger, says "we always get what we need." But why am I listening to him when he can't get no (grammar, grammar!) satisfaction and I have multiples. This leads to the real lessons that change our destiny, attitude and relationships.

OUR LIFE LESSONS ARE TO ATTEMPT TO GIVE UP

Judgements

Expectations

Comparisons

Need to Understand.

Understanding is the booby prize. *I* have to keep working on that one. "How can the bum do such a thing?" "How could she, after she promised...? I do not understand." Ms. Jan! What is ... is.

Change does happen, accepting it is another matter.

The hurt is disguised as anger and is in the cellular level. The depth of the hurt comes from a deeper place, the place called Fear. Anger is frequently the cover for fear and hurt. Underneath that, there will be some grieving whether for declining health, a dear person or a dream lost.

Be clear that some people will not show up when you believe you need them most. Often it is not out of selfishness or not caring. We may never know what is in someone's heart. Usually it is their own issue, having nothing to do with us. "Gee, after all I did for..." We need to realize that the giving is not matched or balanced by receiving. They are both sides of the same coin. Often our own need to give is actually mixed in with our need to receive.

Acceptance and *Allowance* must happen to change anything. First, recognize who you are and where you are in this process. Whatever our issue, the goal is to get to *Acceptance,* and that requires time.

Under the need to control, to lose control, to be strict, to be lax, to be obsessively neat, to clutter, to overeat, to starve oneself, to over-drink or drug or fanatically use religion or any other extreme need, one must first say: "I accept this about myself. I do not like it. I do not want it. I want to change it. Yet I am unable to do so at this time." But it is what it is. That is *Acceptance.* Once we come to this, it gets easier. But, sister, getting to this is the part that is difficult.

We absolutely do not like this quality about ourselves so why would we accept it? Because we are seeing this only on the human level. In the spiritual realm, there is no judgment about any of our flaws. Indeed, there are no flaws. It is simply energy. Like a light bulb which can brighten a church or a brothel, energy has no judgment either way. So guilt, that most useless emotion of all, or blame or any other critical analysis of others or ourselves has no place except when it is followed by truth-telling about what it is we are actually needing and can learn from the hurt.

The job is to get to that in ourselves. Transforming the disappointment in ourselves into accepting that we are mortals and being gentle and loving with ourselves starts the transformation. I have heard that in India blankets are woven with one flaw. The reason: only God (or Martha S.) is perfect! Whew, that sure takes the burden off me!!!

Make a declaration: "This is the way I live. Okay, I do not like it. There is more than this." Practice talking with the soul: "Talk to me, tell me." The soul is different from the personality. The personality is totally ego and the false us. How we appear to others in our mind and what we do or say to look good to them is not our genuine self. The outside world will never know you. Your soul knows. You know.

The second step in *Acceptance* allows us to see things from a different perspective. Need is different from desire. Once we get away from the "need" for "them" to understand us or the circumstance, we can say, "It is my desire, but I do not need that from others." We are free. It is always the "need" that is false.

Others may never "get us." Accepting is part of this. Accepting is acting from a *higher place*. When issues come from NEED, it is the child's need and hurt in us that are being acted out. Now that some of us are swinging seniors (okay, one out of two at least), we do not need others' approval. (But still, would it kill you to say something nice?)

I came to experience it all. The goal is: I know who I am. (Though sometimes I need my name tag to remember.) All the rest is need. When we know who we truly are, what others think, feel or say cannot affect us. So, am I that tall thin blonde that I'm always talking about? Oh, wait. That is someone else! Hey! I'm a senior. Sometimes I forget. Gimme a break, dude!

Just when I serenely became the Queen of Acceptance over my past losses and was up for a Nobel Prize, I developed a

Meningioma Brain Tumor. The talented Sheryl Crow and I have much in common except that I can't sing a note. True, in spite of that, I did teach Edith Bunker how to sing. And music came in handy during child rearing. When my kids were naughty, I threatened to sing if they did not behave. They would beg me to beat them instead. Of course, I did neither. But they turned out swell anyway.

As for me, I work on all of the above constantly and fail often. I had the tumor removed, and the surgeon said it was my attitude and humor that brought about rapid healing. As my hair was growing back, my caregiver dyed it platinum. I'd always wondered what it would be like to be a blonde, but I looked like Eminem. Y'know, the rapper. I started to curse, grab my crotch and considered a tattoo saying, "Born to be kinda, sorta, maybe a little bit wild." My hair grew back to mousy brown.

I have added another flaw, I mean *energy*. I used to say "doo-doo" till I was 48 years old. Now, I curse like a truck driver when I see an injustice or cannot open a jar. I like to believe there is no judgment in this. But just in case, since truck drivers are shocked and "tsk, tsk" me a lot, I often wash my mouth out with soap and send myself to bed without dessert. That will teach me!

HAPPY ENDINGS!

(My will and testiness)

25

MY NEXT-TO-LAST WILL AND TESTAMENT

(While I Am of Sound Mind and So-So Body)

First of all, I want to know the truth before we start with all the details. I want to make plans. I do not want surprises and end up at Saint Peter's gate where he tells me my name and password do not match.

Tell me the absolute truth if something is malignant or there are complications. Do not spare me. Even if there is a worst-case scenario, I want to know, as this will allow me to plan and complete certain matters, which will include eating two pizzas and a whole Sara Lee Pound cake with Nutty Peanut Butter.

If something serious occurs where I am incapacitated for a *while*, I would rather be in a care facility in Malibu or near that area so it is easier to visit. Or better yet, make plans for me in Hawaii.

However, if I am going to be a vegetable (Broccoli I don't mind but not Brussels sprouts), pull the plug. That means if I cannot do anything like speak, move, think or communicate, I do not want to keep living in that manner. Discuss it among yourselves if you all do not agree. Of course, if you are having a really bad day or hit a lot of traffic on the way to see me, perhaps you should stay out of the decision-making for the moment.

Donate all my organs that are usable to those who most need them. That includes my cellulite to Heidi Klum.

At the celebration of my life, please have the Good Humor Man ring his bell and give the group anything they want.

For the obituary, say, "Jan Marshall leaves her wonderful children, gorgeous, brilliant grandkids and dishes in the sink.

HAVE A GOOD NIGHT!

THE ONLY WAY TO LIVE!

26

LIVING À LA CARTE

It was an ordinary day. I was dining with a friend. The menu read like a situation comedy: Liver Come Back to Me, Goldie Lox and the Three Eggs, Ike and Tina Tuna (a split and stale sandwich) and more.

We settled on a bit of caviar and chilled white wine. Quite luxurious we felt, though simple. I gave the order to our waiter.

"So what do you want as your main course?" he asked.

"This is our main course," I answered.

"But that is just an appetizer. Is that all you're going to eat?"

"That's it, sir, and please bring us a few slices of thin pumpernickel with …"

"An appetizer comes with crackers and only crackers. Order the complete meal and you can get good bread like French, rye or Parker rolls and a lot of good stuff." He was pleading.

"Do you not have pumpernickel bread?" I asked sweetly.

"Yes. But not with the dinner or the caviar appetizer."

"Do you serve corn beef sandwiches?"

Déjà vu. I flashed to Jack Nicholson in *Five Easy Pieces.*

"Yes."

"Are they served on pumpernickel bread if requested?"

"Yes, they are, but…"

"So listen. Instead of putting the pumpernickel on a corned beef sandwich we do not want, bring us a few slices of pumpernickel and hold the corned beef. Okay?"

"Okay, but I'll have to charge you," he said.

"Fine." With that we'd also like a chopped hard-boiled egg, thin slices of onion…"

"We don't have hard-boiled eggs."

"Do you," I asked in my Joan of Arc voice, "serve egg salads?"

"Yes," he replied cautiously.

"Then there is a good chance you may have hard-boiled eggs on the premises as that is what egg salads are made with. Wouldn't you agree?"

"Okay. But I still think the better deal would have been the dinner. All this will probably cost just as much."

That depends on what you mean by cost, I thought.

Our food was served. My friend and I had an exquisite lunch, and it did not cost as much as two complete meals. But that is not the point. We ate *à la carte*. We did not *have* to have the basket of assorted breads. Nor did we choose a salad with choice of Roquefort, oil and vinegar or creamy French dressing. We did not ingest the sinful dessert that would have ultimately landed on our butts. Oh, how virtuous we felt! We were not obliged to accept any coffee or *crème de menthe*.

We ate only what we wanted and with much satisfaction. No more "I don't need the calories but it is already paid for" guilt.

That's when it happened, like a cartoon light bulb going on. Not just another metaphor drifting through my mind and dissipating like cooked alcohol, but a genuine "AHA" experience.

Eating à la carte.

Working à la carte.

Loving à la carte.

Parallels sprang forth full-grown.

All along we tend to accept life's "complete dinners" for the one or two items we really want, while letting someone else put together the rest.

How often do we stay in a relationship that provides security, for example, or protection from the fear of loneliness, but then neglect or destroy so much else of what we need to sustain our very souls?

How frequently have we continued in careers that are draining and devoid of true fulfillment that preclude "living our bliss," just because of the money?

Over and over we take the whole meal because we fail to see our full range of choices, just as we forget how much better we feel when we make those choices ourselves.

Women have historically made changes only after experiencing a major trauma. It seems to take a divorce, a death of a partner, a life-threatening illness or a betrayal of a sacred trust to finally force us into a re-evaluation of our lives, sometimes with less time left in that life than we had hoped for. It is far better to ask oneself this very minute and on a continuing basis:

If I knew I had only a short time to live:

a) Is there anything I need to say now to anyone?

b) Would I stay with my partner?

c) Am I doing the work I love?

d) Am I really listening and following my inner truth?

While having choices was not new to us, the force of the revelation at that time in that place seemed to have a profound effect. Was it one too many waiters, lovers or the mommy in our mind telling us what we could or could not do or be or have?

Does it really matter? It simply happened. We just know that we no longer settle for a feast or a relationship where the side portions are so bitter that they spoil the main dish which we truly desire. We continue to remember that we have options in every situation and interaction. The circumstances we are unable to change we may look at with a different attitude. And… the best part is that we can change our minds anytime, and we do. We are no longer beholden to someone else's version of what is right for us.

A grand banquet awaits us. We can choose all or nothing or anything in-between. Order a Marlon Brandy, Kailua Bankhead or have a Beef Encounter with a new acquaintance.

Accepting whatever whole meal is offered may leave us full but not nourished. "Living *à la Carte*" means filling our days only with "stuff" that is good and satisfying, according to only our own definition of who we are. So my friend, what will YOU have?

TECHNIQUES FOR FEELING GREAT!

27

HEY, WANNA FEEL GOOD IN A HURRY?

If you want to feel completely happy, excited and ecstatic right now, just change your focus. That means to change whatever you are concentrating or thinking that makes you sad, angry, resentful, or any emotion that is ruining this present moment, all you have to do is:

THINK OF AND REMEMBER A TIME WHEN YOU FELT ABSOLUTELY ON TOP OF THE WORLD AND SO VERY HAPPY

Picture it all in vivid detail.

Where was that?

What were you wearing?

Who was there?

Listen to the sounds around you...

Be there now.

Feel your pulse race!

Breathe the way you were breathing.

Put the same expression on your face.

Move your body just as you did then.

Do you feel even a hint of that excitement again?

It is possible that you could feel this way anytime you wish.

GO ON AND DO IT!

ANOTHER TECHNIQUE

TAKE YOUR MIND TO THE MOVIES AND RERUN YOUR SCRIPT

Something happened that pained you? Here is an opportunity to release the angst.

Mentally sit in the theatre. Play the issue from the beginning. "He did that, she said this," and let your mind go over it from the opening to the end of this film.

Immediately re-run this script backwards from the end of your movie to the beginning credits (You were the star and see all the supporting players).

Then play the movie once more.

Re-run it backwards again

Keep doing this several times till the energy is released.

When you play or think of the incident in your movie, it will have little impact. It will simply be a story.

This is all it is, anyway!

TIPS

• PRETEND YOU ARE A HUMOR COLUMNIST.

You have to report one funny incident a day. Write it down.

After a while the absurdities will appear constantly. Perhaps you will have so many incidents, you will write a book!

• VIEW YOUR LIFE AS A SITUATION COMEDY.
  Who would you cast as your family, your boss and yourself as the star and lead character?
  Are you simply too busy at work to do this? Then...

• IMAGINE WOODY ALLEN (OR YOUR FAVORITE COMIC)
  IS FILMING AND STARRING IN YOUR LIFE.
  What would it look like now?

• SET A TIME FOR YOUR MISERY.
  Okay, time's up!

• SING YOUR PROBLEM IN A MUSICAL STYLE.
  Choose: Blues, Country, Jazz, Rock an Roll, Opera, Hip Hop or a Classic.

And while you are at it:

• CHANGE YOUR PHYSIOLOGY, WHICH WILL CHANGE
  YOUR MOOD.
So:
Stand up.
Look up.
Move, Dance and Shake Your Booty, Babe!

Finally:

ALWAYS REMEMBER TO CARRY YOUR KAZOO WITH YOU.

A FINAL THOUGHT

In the fabric of our existence, there are *threads* of pain and sorrow and major disappointments. Still, after we deal and heal each interlude, the truth is these are just threads in a fully-lived life. In-between some of these almost unbearable realities, the truth is, "NOT A SHRED OF EVIDENCE *EXISTS* THAT LIFE IS SERIOUS!"

Jan Marshall

MEET JAN

ABOUT THE AUTHOR

As a Humor Columnist, Certified Clinical Hypnotherapist and motivational speaker, Jan Marshall founded the "International Humor & Healing Institute" in 1986. Prominent physicians and other board members, including Norman Cousins, Steve Allen and Dr. Bernie Siegel, shared her techniques for healing through hope and humor.

She hosted her own television series and was a guest on hundreds of radio and television shows.

Jan regularly appeared on Steve Allen's radio show and he was a guest on her television show as well.

A cancer and brain tumor survivor, she returns with another humorous satirical book, "Dancin Shmancin with the Scars," writing about "Graying and Giggling in the age of Googling." Her first book was "Still Hanging in There ... Confessions of a Totaled Woman."

Jan is a humor columnist for *Senior Correspondent*, *Friends of the Village*, and several Internet magazines.

LAUGHTER HEALS AND CONNECTS US

SPEAKING AND MEDIA

"Your humorous talk on 'Lightening up in the Bedroom and the Boardroom' was one of our liveliest presentations. We left feeling lighter at heart and enlightened as well."

ARCO

"Your wonderful lighthearted approach to relieving problems and stress had great impact on our doctors, nurses and staff. We in the health profession often forget that we do have options. And we had fun!"

CHART

"This is the third time you have appeared at our course 'Humor and Creative Management.' The students picked your presentation as the highlight of the entire experience. Outstanding! Come back again."

UNIVERSITY OF REDLANDS

MISSION STATEMENT

"Humor as a universal language promotes rapport among individuals. It has the potential, along with art, athletics and music in creating a liaison between people, perhaps the ultimate common denominator. Through shared laughter we will bring about our global purpose of caring for one another."

Jan Marshall, Founder of the International Humor & Healing Institute, 1986.

APPRECIATION

IT TAKES A VILLAGE AND MORE THAN
THAN A TEAM OF WILD HORSES...

In addition to attitude and laughter, in order to stay in the dance with life, one needs support teams of all kinds. A partial list of those who come into our space to assist or teach us lessons are our families, friends, medical people of all kinds, personal assistants, financial advisors, caregivers, past lovers, computer experts, dressmakers, attorneys and writing pals and exercising ones and so many more in all situations that have been part of my own personal journey.

The following pages include just some of you who have touched my heart and enriched my life in various ways. I say "thank you" to all.

FAMILY, FAMILY, FAMILY THE BEST FAMILY

Matt Marshall, my first son; a gentle, philanthropic man with universal peace and music as his primary theme in life. He named his first hugely successful music company, "Higher Octave" which he is, as well, in this world. By the way he started the company in our garage. He has always been there for me in so many ways (see the Touched by an Angel Chapter) and seems to be that way with just about everyone including being generous and a caring dad to my first only and special grandson, Syef Folse also a gentle, loving man to his own Sage.

Juliette Marshall, my daughter. I am always astounded by her beauty inside and out. Talented as a writer and comedienne-actress she created and even wrote the music, a new thing, for her hysterically funny and truthful one woman shows. She is so courageous and a fabulous mom to our Hana. Together we sometimes make a goofy pair and are often asked to leave a Restaurant. What can I say! We seem to find humor where other people do not.

David Marshall, youngest son; a brilliant entrepreneur and business man like his dad. He is such a caring father to his daughters the adorable and talented sweeties, Shanti and Sedona. He is super husband to his Neidda who herself, is a gourmet cook, a patient and progressive mom and..President of the PTA

Sid Marshall, Father to these siblings and my loving husband for a quarter of a century. A brilliant Advertising genius and generous man, adored by his children and still by me, though we both have moved on.

Hana Joy Marshall-Trattner, Stunning, brilliant, kind and my first granddaughter, thanks to Juliette and Jim. So smart and my friend...I mean she did friend me on Face Book! Along with her Mama Juliette, we three can get kind of goofy together. I like that legacy

Fred Kellerman my incredible brother. He is so funny and kindhearted; a computer genius and so good through and

through. Along with his wife Helen, they are the entertaining gurus of all time.

Dynese Kellerman Addotta is my brave niece, counselor and good friend along with her gorgeous girls Gina and Nicole who have made her a grandma at a very young age.

Debra Kellerman De Shon, a remarkable woman, was a surrogate mom for an infertile couple and regular mother to many including Freddy named after his grand pop. Caring step mom to others, she trains dogs for the government and the disabled. How about that!

Aunt Esther Milgram, Still wants me to call her auntie even though I am almost her age. She continues to be funny and lovely, though lonely without her sweet Hoibital, but a card game soothes that, temporarily.

Phillip Milgram, MD, a ladies doc and my Buddy in La Jolla. We have been favorite cousins from the beginning

Sheri Milgram Goncher A gorgeous, talented and brilliant woman and so nice. I wish she lived next door.

Jim Trattner, Dad to Hana and my ex son in law who is still a friend. Can you believe it? He wrote such a lovely tribute to me on LinkedIn. I mean really, I am his EX mother-in law! Isn't that against the law?

Sandra Hay, Matt's partner and my heart sister. Another treasure came into my life through my son Matthew, that most supportive being and kind heart; his sweetheart Sandra Hay whom I consider both a daughter and friend. What a perfect match since they are both humanitarians to the highest degree! Matthew, through his devoted involvement with Earthdance, the universal peace group and Sandra who brings spirit and light to my life and to the rest of the world. She is founder of UnseenPictures which are documentaries that enrich and change the world and are actually seen all over the planet, enriching lives. Change the name to SeenALot Pictures, babe.

Catherine Curry and Zan (Alexander)…former loves in Matt's world who remain immersed in my heart. He really knows how to pick them. I truly miss them.

Murray (Doc) Greenspan Yippie! My long lost favorite cousin from Brooklyn whom I have recently found and his wife Carol. Murray and I have so much in common politically spiritually and in methods of healing we could be twins, though he likes camping and I like hotels. He owns the Greenspan Chiropractic Clinic in North Carolina, how did he get there… with his children who are Chiropractors as well and considered the best in the Carolinas and all surrounding states.

THE BOOK GURUS

Anne Clark, the beautiful computer expert and gentle uplifting soul who turned a bunch of words into electronic and printed miracles. I think if I brought her a bowl of Alphabet soup she could rearrange it into a best seller. She truly know her stuff!!

Charles Clark, talented computer maven and sweet support.

Lucy V Parker, an established author and print editor and oh-so-kind associate and friend in putting the book together and sipping Margaritas.

Karli Jessen of Style{d} by Karli The Social Networking genius who accomplished magic from mush.

Paul Kirby – Video expert

Drew Shepard – Apple Expert

AND THE TALENTED BOOK COVER DESIGNER AND DEAR, DEAR FRIEND, STANLEY FRIEDMAN

JULIE SEBESTYEN, OF JULIE'S SUPER SERVICE
Sometimes good surprises come with bumps in the head.

When I needed a caregiver for my brain surgery gig, during and after the cut, the best care giver in the world, Julie Sebestyen knocked on the door and danced on my heart.

The hardest worker I know is my Julie. A single mom for 16 years she earnestly and lovingly brought up her son Tommy to be a fine (and handsome) young man. Recently she married a true treasure who been her friend for years, Billy Rennie. They finally confessed they had always had been a little in love with

one another. I love that story. I am happy to say, I danced at her wedding. There is a kindness and loyalty to Julie that is treasured by me and those who know her. Anyone fortunate enough to have her care for them, or anyone else from her fabulous staff (always supervised by Julie), became a fan for life.

Julie's Super Services provides exactly that. Not only caring for your health but completing many chores a person, home and office could ever need.

She is our supreme senior advocate and partner in all things Chocolate. Thank you, Julie, for making my life that much sweeter.

DR JARED ZEFF Naturopathic Physician
We are old friends; well I am older anyway, from Los Angeles. He provides support in any way needed and is one of the gentlest healing souls of the world; a man I am proud to call an associate as well. I presented several humor segments at a seminar he designed for Northwest physicians. At first they were so resistant to be taught how to lighten up for themselves and to benefit their patients and then...they turned into unruly junior high school hooligans in a good way. I never laughed so much myself. When no other healing application works for your illness, it is worth the trip to the Salmon Clinic in Vancouver Washington where miracles will occur with Jared, in a non toxic and supportive manner. I love this man. You will too. And he will make you healthy again!

Bernice Schachter, brilliant sculptor, artist and teacher. My movie buddy and dear, dear friend who has never uttered an unkind word. A former President of our Local Pen Women association she has always supported the arts and all humans who come across her path though has now fallen in love with her doggie. Her sculpture stands in front of the National League of American Pen Woman in Washington. Though in her mid eighties, she is now designing jewelry and teaching others as well. Wowie!

Tom Pontac is my best male buddy. We met while at Fatburgers when I was trying to boost my blood count before surgery. I gave him my number which I never do; even the telephone company doesn't have it; and we have been buds since then. He is always there for me and I for him which is so endearing for both of us. He brought me hamburgers from you know where during my Chemo treatments and wrote me the loveliest, funniest poems. He is in fact, one of the foremost wittiest poets around. He and his wife Jeanie run marathons which they started as seasoned citizens and together make one darling, active couple.

MY SUPPORT TEAM IN GENERAL

Selina Forfar: so adorable, organized, kind and so very helpful.

Anna and Greg Gorcycza: Teachers in Poland helpers and friends in Laguna.

Neil Grimwood. If it is broken, he will fix it, paint it or haul it and he does it all with such a sweet attitude.

Gigi Michaels, where for art thou, most efficient gal I have ever known? We learned the computer together while she ran my business, my home and my relocations and now she runs her own computer consulting company as a single mom and has returned to graduate school as well. She has been through the worst challenges and still continues on and looks great. How does she do that? I want what she's having!!!!

Ryan Michaels, my pal in Washington, with his wheel chair, rolls around the halls of congress as an intern but is destined for greater things like being a standup comic. Well, a comic anyway.

Cliff Michaels, an extremely positive man and motivator. He is the author of the "4 Essentials of Entrepreneurial Thinking."

N Taylor Collins is an artist extraordinaire with a specialty in folk art though she has expanded into many areas. As an author she appeared in three anthologies and is awaiting publication of her newest work. As the former National President in Washington of the National League of American Pen Women she continues to support others through motivational speaking and just being witty and creative. When she went back into the dating game she asked my advice. I told her not to wear a wedding dress on the first date and she didn't. Now she has a great fella. See, you got questions; I got answers. Taylor and I may write a dating manual for immature mature women when we stop giggling.

Suellen Zima, author of "Memoirs of a Middle-aged Hummingbird" which is about her travels as an American teacher exploring the world independently and going to villages where a white woman had never been before, would rather travel than do anything else. However, she is hovering long enough to be local president of the Laguna Beach Pen Women group where she almost single handedly takes care of us all.

Maryann Goldberg

Owns and runs the yummy Kosher Bite Deli for our delight. When a pastrami sandwich is the only thing I crave, I go to Maryann. She says laughter is the second best thing to Chicken soup, and I say only if the soup is cooked at the Kosher Bite!

♥

Eleanor Roosevelt said, "Many people will walk into your life but only true friends will leave footprints in your heart"

Here are but a few of you (and some places, that I can recall). If your name is not here, remember that brain tumor incident — sometimes I do forget momentarily (I just love having an excuse) so please contact me and I will mention you in my next book, "I Forgot to Remember to Remind You to Forget Me!"

Adapt to It
Addision Arthur
Adrienne Shanks
Advanced Physical Therapy Staff
Al, Alice and Henry Howard
Alex Kroll
All my Friends of the Village
All the women at WOWoWOW
Allan Sosin, MD
Anderson Cooper
Allison Abbott
AlterMax
Amazon
American Brain Tumor Association
American Cancer Society
Andy Vizvary
Anita Cohen Pasteur
Ann Britt
Annabelle Furgerson
Anne Reeves
Anne Wallburger
Annella Keene

Anthony Robbins
Ashley "Supercut" Calabasas
Augie Haboush
Babs Morris
Baby Boomers of Laguna Woods, all my friends there.
Bahar Sedarati, MD
Barbara Goldberg
Barbara Hayden, MD
Barbara Herzog
Barbara Bubbles Breit
Barbara De Angeles
Barbara Lee
Barbara Potter
Barnes and Noble
Becky Tauber
Bernie Siegel, MD
Bernie Weitzman
Beverly Long
Bill Harris
Bill McFadden
Bing
Bloomie's
Bob Basso
Bob Thompson
Bobbie and Burt Bilson
Bobby Bliven
Brendon Buchard
Bronwyn Jones
Brook Burman,

Brooke, Audiologist Extraordinaire
Brooklyn
Bunny Sussman
Burbank
Buzz Belmondo
California News
Candace Wheeler
Carine Nadel
Carl and Estele Reiner
Carol Anne Kraft
Carol Burnett
Carol Feldman
Carol Hemingway
Carol Kivaz
Carol Swanson
Carole Garland
Cedars Sinai Hospital
Charlene Rechenberg
Chris McKerracher
Clara Obsushin
Cliff from Viewcrest
Conley Falk
Craig Gelfand
Dan Levine
Dan MacEachern
Dan Poynter
Dana and Sunny Nail Chateau
Daniel Hall
Daniel McCullou

Deana Windham, MD
Deb Reed
Debbie Tideman
Deborah Perdue
Debra Angeletti
Debra Fine
Debra Gomez
Denise Frazer
Denny (Best Senior Activist) Welch
Diana NewKirk
Diana Von Welanetz Wentworth
Diane Perkins Frazen
Diane Zwang
Dior Salon
DivineCaroline
Dizzyland Dr. Mango
Dolly Mc Garry
Donna Cowan
Doralyn Folse
Doris Kalmenson
Dorothy Parker
Dr. Wang
Dr. Wayne Dyer
Dr. Wong
Drew Leder, PhD
Drew Shepard
Dwight Moody
Eddie Kole
Editors Mary Robertson, Pat Wilkenson and Marion Daily

Edna Reid
Elephant Bar
Elisa Hirsh
Elise Lane
Elizabeth Hanratty
Ellen Reid
Estelle Reiner
Eve Breir
Eve Friedman
Evy Asher Tannenberg
FaboverFifty
Family Circle
Francis Halpern
Gabriel Dery, MD
Gail Brockman, MD
Gail King
Gail McNulty
Garelick, Wilkerson and Brooks
Garry Marshall
Gary Henderson
Gene Hackler
Gerald Schnitzer
Ghislain Viau
Google
Grace Chang, MD
Guillermo Riviera
Gutsy Indie Publishers
Haircutters Pam, Carmen, Denise and Jackie
Hap Pattiz

Harry "from the Bronx" Obsushin
Helena Carter
Helen Raptis
Henny Youngman
Henry J Kaiser
Hillary Clinton
Hollywood
Honey Henderson
Huffington Post
Humor Writers
Hyla Cass, MD
Inside Edge friends
iPhone, IPad, Mac, Apple
Jack Canfield
Jacob Blass
James Maynard
Jan Anderson
Jane Hamilton
Janie McGuire
Jay Gattis, PhD
Jayne Meadows
Jean Kasem
Jennifer Speckland
Jerry Beckerman
Jerry Engle
Jerry Lynch
Jerry McFadden
Jerry Shanks
Jessica Cassady, Ph.d

Jo Ann Bonot

Joe Casey

John (the Cork) McCorcoran

John Cleese

John Draper

John Merino, DDS

John Sweetland

Jon Noel

Jon Tandler

Josh Tauber

Joy Schary

Joyce and Jay Leanse

Joyce Schwarz

Joyce Simpson Dove

JS Frager

Judith Briles

Judith Chips

Judy Chaiken

Judy Holliday

Judy Pazanti

Judy Rich

Judy Stone

Julian Han

Julian Whittaker, MD

Julie Wilkerson

Juliette's friend Melissa

June Brooks

Karen G Jackovich

Karen Gonzales

Karina Nilsen

Kasey Kasem

Kathy Irwin, Phillip and Lee Lai

Kathy Plomaritis

Katie Couric

Katy Truskin-Veadov

Kay Tosti @ Chicos

Ken Cowan

Ken Goldenberg

Ken Harrison

Ken Pucci

Kim Delaney

Kim Sherek

LA Magazine

LA Times

Ladies Who Lunch

Laguna Beach NLAPW all of you

Laguna Niguel MRI

Laguna Woods Writer's Club all of you, too

Larry Lipson

Larry Strauss

Laura Maloney and THE Wonderful Jean

Letty Norris

Lexus South County, Mission Viejo, CA

Lillian Lipson

Linda Ellerbee

Lindken Group

Linton Robinson

Lisa Michaels

Lloyd Zackary
Lolly Ortiz
Lord Mayor Ben Briscoe
Lori Olsen,
Lorraine Jossel
Los Angeles Magazine
Lou Garelick
Louise Chamis
Lucia Foster
Lulu Milgram
LW Billiards
LW Comedy Club
LW Gym
LW Mac Club
LW PC Club
LW Rock n Roll Club
LW Writer's Club Pals
Lydia and Derek Forfar
Macy's
Malcolm Kam
Malibu
Mallory Flynn, my editor at Senior Correspondents
Marc Bachrach
Marcus Laux, MD
Marilyn Heisner
Marilyn Miller
Mark Chimsky
Mark Plomaritis, Laura and Ashley, too
Mark Twain

Mark Weiss
Martha Beck
Martin Perleberger
Marty Franks
Marv Rosenhaft
Mary Jo Hirsch
Mayor Larry Agran
Mel Brooks
Memorial Hospital
Michael Goldman, MD
Michael Gorczyca
Michael Now
Michael Wilkerson
Michelle Mitzel
Michelle Wallerstein
Mike Edge
Mike Koenig
Millie Brown
Moe Friedman
Moishe Zwang,
More Magazine
Mothers Market
Moulton Pharmacy
My entire "Showbiz Show" crew from WIF
National League of American Pen Woman pals
New JC Penney
New York Times
Newport Audiology
Nikki Koenig Goldberg

Nikki Leskowitz
Noel Hatch
Nora Ephron
Norm Salzberg
Norman Cousins
Norman Heisner
Norman Horowitz
Norton Wright
O. Carl Simonton, MD
Otto Rechenberg
Pamela Shandel
Pat Kirk
Patricia Ballard
Patricia Moody
Patti Figueroa
Paul Campbell
Paul Kirby
Paul Konopasky
Paul Ortiz
Peggy Blizzard
Penny Cluttercleaner
Peter Konopasky
Philomena Mc Andrews, MD
Phyllis Diller
Phyllis London
Prudence Broadwell, MD
Rick Frishman
Rob Merritt
Rob Truskin

Robby Frishman
Robert Carlin, MD
Robert Jackson, MD
Roberta and David Berk
Roger Sorenson
Rona Edwards
Rona Jeffrey
Ronnie Kay
Rose Kapler
Rupert Macnee
Russell Fine
Ruth Avergon
Ryan Cassaday
Saddleback Hospital
Sally Michaels
Sandra Church
Sandy Clayton
Santa Monica Hospital
Saverio and Rosemary
Schur & Sugarman
Scott Frishman
Senior Correspondents
Shannon Ricci
Sharon Edwards
Sheila Kramer Mc Canna
Sheila Wilkerson
Sheila Wright
Sheri Goncher
Sherry Lansing

Sierra Buchanan
Soft Surroundings
Sonia Marsh
Stan Corwin
Stanley Friedman
Starbucks
Steve Allen, Jr. MD
Steve Edwards
Steve Harrison
Studio City
Sue Crawford
Sue Priver
Susan Jeffers
Susan Levine
Susan Nessin
Susan Watson
Susan Wright
Suzy Mallery
Suzy Rosenberg
Sylvana Martino, MD
Sylvester Center
Tanspersonal Hypnotherapist Institute Alumni Pals
Tim Allen
Tim Piering
Timothy Hurley
Toby (Selwyn) Tauber
Tommy Sebestyn
Toni Galardi
Tony Raynor

Tracy Beer
Tracy Meehan
Trader Joe's
UN Women
Valley Green Sheet
Valley Magazine
VB Wilson
Verna Schneider PS 165
Viewcrest Road
Wall St. Journal
Walt Wood
Wellness Community
Whole Foods
Women In Film
Woody Allen
Young & Rubicam friends
Zack, Lover and Friend
Ben Franklin
TV STATIONS & ENTERTAINERS:
ABC
CBS
CNN
COMEDY CHANNEL
David Letterman
Discovery
Ellen Degeneres
Entertainment Tonight
Gail and Larry King
Good Morning America

Jay Leno
Jimmy Fallon
Jimmy Kimmel
Johnny Carson
Jon Stewart
Ladies of the View
MSNBC
NBC
OPRAH
Steve Allen
Today Show
The View Ladies
EXTRA SPECIAL PLACES:
HAWAII, EUROPE, JAMAICA, MALIBU, MALIBU AND
MALIBU, MANHATTAN, PARIS, TOPANGA, LAUREL
CANYON, MAINE, LONDON, VERMONT, VENICE,
PARADISE COVE, SANTA BARBARA, SANTA MONICA
AND LA JOLLA, CA
Currently, I cannot place all the names with faces.
If we ever met, you touched my heart in some manner
So, I appreciate you as well! JM

35823494R00100

Made in the USA
San Bernardino, CA
06 July 2016